Life of Abuse
TO SUCCESS:
"A Child's Story"

Life of Abuse
TO SUCCESS:
"A Child's Story"

Walter Lawrence

Kravitz & Sons
INNOVATORS IN PUBLISHING, MARKETING AND ADVERTISING

Kravitz and Sons LLC
1301 Farmville Blvd, Suite 104
Greenville, NC 27834

Published by Kravitz and Sons LLC.

ISBN: 979-8-89639-241-5 (sc)
ISBN: 979-8-89639-242-2 (e)

Library of Congress Control Number:

1 was born in 1946. When I was six years old, our family moved to New Jersey where my father drove a city bus. I remember playing in the front yard as my grandmother was chasing my mother out the front door with a knife in her hand. I never found out why, but my brother and sister, who were twins, were about two years old, and I was six years old. I'm guessing my mother was not caring for them as she should, which would have angered my grandmother.

In 1952 we moved to California by way of five-day road trip to the City of Hope, City of Pasadena and San Bernadino, California. From the ages of six through nine, I went to four different elementary schools between 1952 to 1955. In late 1954 we lived in San Bernadino and during the ages of seven through nine I played the accordion at local fairs and the Mission Playhouse, which was a historical building. I still have a photo of me with red hair and freckles, and I looked like Howdie Doodie. One day a neighbor knocked on the door. The twins had gotten a hold of paint in the neighbor's garage and painted graffiti around the entire outer walls of the garage about three feet high up from the ground.

In the summer of 1955 my brother, Wayne, who was five at the time, acquired walking pneumonia. He got sick on a Friday night. My mother went in the ambulance with him to Los Angeles Medical Center. My father followed later with myself and my sister. As we arrived at the hospital, my mother ran down the hall and said, "he is gone." My father and I started crying, and he started pacing up and down the hall. He was hysterical. That's where I found out where my brother's body was, and my father lifted me up to show him to me with his lifeless body and eyes wide open. He was five years old in 1955 before my brother passed, I used to clean out Morgan horse stalls for one dollar a month on a ranch. I was eight and a half years old. I don't know why he thought that was important or why he did that, but on the day of the funeral, I chose to go to the horse ranch instead.

At the age of eleven I went to Jone's Beach with my mother on Long Island, NY. At that time and place there weren't any lifeguards. I went into the water and the waves were very, very high and calm with an outgoing tide.

I was sucked out by the high waves to a point where my mother on the beach looked like a dot on the sand. "How do I get back to the beach?" I asked myself. I then decided with calm high waves I would get to the top of the wave and swim down each one and wait for the next one and then do the same. I must have done this over twentyfive times and finally reached the shore, not even my mother knew this was happening to me. Amazing to me I kept myself calm, saving my own life.

In October of 1955 we moved back to Brooklyn, New York, where I attended fifth and sixth grade at P.S. 102. My nana cleaned the houses of my teachers. I was never given any special attention, and I did what I had to do to pass. Next was seventh grade, and we moved again, this time out of the district, and I attended junior high school at McKinley Junior high. I had a teacher named Mrs. Macgiveny. There were gangs in the school, and there was so much disruption that I was glad I was only there three months. In the summer of 1957, one of my enjoyments in the parks was catching butterflies with my net and then mounting them in picture frames. They were Tiger Swallows, Monarchs, and Moths, which was called Lepidopterology. You use a container with a wet sponge and then place a piece of glass under and over each wing spreading them out like they were soaring. The glass would prevent the smearing of the powdered wing pattern. In the summer my mother will give me twenty-five cents, and I would take the 69th St Ferry to Staten Island. It cost five cents to ride the ferry at that time. After the ferry ride, I would walk up the hill to the Saint George public swimming pool and outside was a hot dog stand. It was ten cents for a hot dog. I got into the pool for five cents and swam for the afternoon and took the ferry back with my last five cents. So, for twenty-five cents I had a ferry ride, a hot dog and an afternoon swim. I wasn't sure if these twenty-five cents were her way of caring or if it was to just get me out of the way. I'd like to think it was her way of caring.

I had a red flyer wagon, and I would visit apartment houses, empty the dumb waiters of newspapers, load up my red wagon and take them to the junkie. I would get twenty-five cents per 100 pounds. Once a month I would take a drop line and a sinker and dip the sinker in a tin cup with axle grease and then lay on my stomach on the subway grates and send the sinker on the drop line down and collect all the coins the churchgoers had dropped in front of the churches.

I also remember a time in 1956 that my father had gone on a fishing trip and got in a rage when my mother was late picking him up because the boat got back an hour early and he had to take a cab home.

Around 1958 in Brooklyn, I went to F.W. Woolworth's department store and while in there, I took a candy bar off the shelf and didn't pay for it. In 1973 while visiting my nana, I went back to the same store and bought the same bar of candy after paying for it and put the candy back on the shelf.

At the end of that school year, we moved to Queens, New York where my father purchased a delicatessen, and I started at a Lutheran Elementary (my seventh school).

During that time after my brother died and up until 1963, every time my mother had a bad day, she would beat me for no reason. I noticed a big change in my parents' mental states after my brother's death. On his deathbed In 1973 on Memorial Day, my father told me that there had been no intimacy between my mother and him since the death of my brother. That day my nana who was always there to protect me, secretly gave me a few twenty-five dollar savings bonds dated from 1956 through 1970 valued at about $5,000. I decided to cash them in and was told they are P.O.D. So, I gave them back to my nana to cash them in in 1977. After her funeral, I asked my mother about my bonds and she said to me, "you lose". I was then asked to go to her apartment and clean it out by my mother's half-brother Paul. So I got my brother in law at the time and we removed the furniture and stuff and found a jar of coins that must have had about fifty dollars in nickels, dimes, and quarters in it. I had borrowed a truck from a friend, took a day off from work, paid the landfill fees and for the fuel we used. I split the coins with my sister when I got home. My mother's brother found out about the coins and was furious because we kept the coins. It was his mother, and he never offered any type of reimbursement for doing that.

From 1960 through 1964, I went to Martin Luther High School. In 1962 my father had a nervous breakdown and went to the VA hospital for three months. I remember right before this happened my father had a meltdown and tried to attack me while I was working as a clerk in the deli. During High School in 1963, I had basketball practice twice a week and my father would complain because I couldn't work in the deli with him on those days, so I decided to quit the team. He got mad at me then because I wasn't on the team. I always felt that I couldn't satisfy either parent with anything that I did. After he tried to attack me in the deli, I ran off to my nana's house in Brooklyn, arriving there about 1:00am for sanctuary. I woke up on her couch and my father had come to pick me up. I don't know what my nana said to him that day on the phone, but from then on, all the abuse stopped. I feel like I raised myself without any parental love that a parent gives their children.

"To be at the right place at the wrong time."

In 1962 my father and I took a three-day trip to Bermuda. My mother stayed back to run the deli business while we were gone. The hotel had a pool. I played golf and rode mopeds with my father. The second evening we went to dinner and there was a lady sitting at our table. When we left, I went to the hotel pool alone. The next day we flew home. About three days later the mail came to the deli with a letter addressed to my father. My mother opened it. It said, "I hope you miss me like I miss you." My mother was furious and questioned me alone about what was going on. I told her I knew nothing, and I didn't because in the evening hours I was alone and amused by myself.

On Friday, November 22, 1963, I cut school and took a subway to Manhattan to Wall St. and Broadway and sat on a cemetery bench in the Trinity Church where the movie National Treasure was made in the 1990's. I realized I didn't have the 15 cents fair to get back home. A man next to me was nice enough to give me 25 cents and I thanked him. This was at 1:00 pm. I tried to time myself to get home at the same time as I would have if I had gone to school. I got off at the Forest Hills station and walked to the candy store to buy candy with the 10 cents I had left from the gentleman who gave it to me. The radio was on in the store, and they announced that John F. Kennedy had been assassinated.at 1:00 pm. This was the same time that I was at Trinity cemetery. I got to my parents' deli and my father was crying and pacing. I then walked 5 stores away to our apartment where my mother was napping. I woke her and told her to go to the deli to console my father.

In 1964, after graduating high school, I joined the service but I was rejected because of a pineal cyst at the tip of my lower spine, which is common In males. I went back home after that. I felt like a lost puppy. No job, knowing that I wasn't loved except by my nana. I needed to find a job and back then there was no internet and only pay phones. It wasn't easy to just come up with a job offer or know where to look first. I had a Corvair in 1965. I was getting into the car to go to an appointment when my father came out of the deli very angry because I had to leave work at the deli. So, he ripped my radio antennae off my car. I was nineteen years old, trying to better myself and get away from the abuse. Another vivide memory is that I never saw my mother or my father smile.

Finally, I went back to my high school principal at Martin Luther High School for help. He had a list of job openings, and I got a job in Manhattan as an office clerk in delivering mail and running errands for Texas Gulf Sulphur in the Pan Am building, which is now the Met Life Building over Grand Central Station in New York City. I worked there for a year making seventy dollars a week. From there I went to an employment agency and got a job with. New York Helicopters serving LaGuardia, JFK, and Newark airports working for New York airways. I met a lot of celebrities.

Cary Grant came out of the TWA terminal in early 1968. Trying to get into his limo but the doors were locked. His chauffeur went inside the terminal by another door looking for Mr. Grant. I approached and he looked startled because he was approached by me. Then he calmed down after I told him where the limo driver went and he thanked me. He was a very shy person in his personal life.

In 1972 Dad and I went to play a round of golf. Another car hit us and dented the fender on the car. When we told my mother she punched me in my testicles. At my parent's home in Wantagh, New York I mowed their lawn on my day off and when my father pulled up in the driveway and had another mental breakdown he reamed me out for getting grass cuttings on the sidewalk on the side of the house before I had time to clean it up. The abuse did keep going on even later when I was twenty years old. I was the whipping boy for their anger that they kept inside them.

During this time (1965-1967) I hooked up with someone I thought was my friend, someone I could love and receive the love that I never received from my parents. We had a child together, a daughter. Her mother and I didn't work out and I had the baby for four months. During a custody battle, I was accused of throwing her mother through a window that was four feet above a kitchen sink. In later years, her mother did admit to our daughter that that never happened to her. That's not the person I am. I would never hit a woman. For some reason there was a lot of tension between her father and I, and I never knew why. My oldest daughter and I reconnected forty years later. She told me that he had another family in

North Carolina where he would go once a month as a fabric salesman.

In the 1970's I married my second wife. She was the youngest of five children. I was twenty-three and she was twenty. Our first daughter was born in 1973. While working at New York Airways, I started a cleaning business to financially keep us afloat from 1973 to 1979. Unfortunately, I was working at the airport from 3:00 pm to 11:00 pm and then cleaned after work and didn't get home until around 1:30 am. While working at the airport for the helicopter service I was asked to escort and carry the luggage of a passenger to the Delta terminal. The passenger was Frank Perdue (the eldest one as in Perdue Chicken). It was a quarter mile walk, and he never talked to me or gave me a tip. I found out later from other people where he lived that he was always a cheap son of a gun.

In 1977 my wife gave birth to a second daughter, who was born with Down's Syndrome. The doctors told us it was a chromosome imbalance in the mother's DNA. That daughter died three months later. In 1979 we lost another child eight weeks prematurely due to complications from an amniocentesis again we were told due to chromosome issues in the mother. I was against the amnio, and we were told the odds of its (Down's) happening again were 1500:1. My ex-wife ignored my advice and had the test anyway. The child was normal except the amnio caused a premature birth. The child died 4 hours later. This was the start of the downfall of the marriage. My daughter and I had a good relationship up until she turned twelve. The marriage ended in the spring of 1985. All of this would tear any marriage apart, but my ex-wife turned our daughter against me with lies and deceit, jealous of my success where she was hoping for my downfall. We divorced in 1985.

In the spring of 1985, while living in Babylon Village on Long Island, I was going through a divorce and living in our house alone after she moved out. I got a call to go to Hauppauge, New York to meet her to see what I thought was a marriage counselor. When I arrived at the complex of many buildings and finally finding the right one, I entered into an auditorium with an elevated stage surrounded by seats. There were thirty or forty people in those seats. On the stage there were four seats for my daughter, my estranged wife, me and the counselor. As I looked to my right there was a room with a window that had the blinds dosed.

The counselor started to ask me questions and the blinds slowly opened and there were twenty or so people seated there observing me, I was asked about my relationship with my daughter. I said I loved her and always tried to give her advice. She was thirteen at the time. I realized at that time that I was not there to be a loving father but to be scrutinized by her mother. I stood up and said to the audience, "shame on all of you." I then walked out. This was the mentality of my ex-wife. She brainwashed my daughter and only a mother with issues of her own would do this. Shame on her. She was trying to use the reverse psychology while she was having an affair with her boss while I was working ten-to-twelve-hour days trying to provide.

My sister and I have had very little contact of the years. I visited her in Oceanside, New York In 1986 and talked to her once on the phone in 2005. She was living in the Shenandoah Valley then. She and her first husband had two children together, but he turned out to be gay. She married her second husband and had two more children. He later committed suicide. Their son named after her dead twin (my brother) had ADHD and was dosed up on Ritalin committed suicide by train at the age of twenty-one in 2001 in Jacksonville, Florida. She married again and with her third husband had another child and I never knew what happened to him. After that marriage ended, she had a boyfriend who stole $25,000 from her credit cards and took off.

A year later I moved from Long Island to Sullivan County, New York. There I drove a school bus and took a civil service test for the Sullivan County Sheriff's Department. In 1991 working from 1:00am to 9:00am for the Times Herald Record, a newspaper in Middletown, New York delivering bulk newspapers. I also went to Sullivan County Community College for a culinary degree. While attending English class I had to write an essay on a food menu item. My essay was titled, "Road Kill". It was about squirrels, turtles, possums, and rabbits. I was forty-four years old in a class with twenty-year olds. I got an A- on the essay. They all asked how I got that grade. I said as you get older your imagination also grows.

I was hired on January 8, 1992, as a corrections officer. There I met my current wife of twenty-six years. She was a jail nurse. We were married in 1999 and built a home on Yankee Lake in Wurtsboro. In 2002 I retired from the Sheriff's Department. We sold the home in 2004 and moved to Citrus County, Florida. I started a thriving lawn business and did that for eleven years. My wife is a hospice nurse, and I now work for the Citrus County Sheriff's Department as a Crossing Guard for the schools.

In the 1950s when the abuse began, I promised myself that I would live my life and never lie or blame anyone for my mistakes. In 2008 my wife and I went up to New York and visited my mother who was in a nursing home. During our conversation she said, "How nice you turned out". She was totally blinded about who I really was. She passed on 12/25/2010 at ninety-one years old.

On a strange note, my wife and I moved into our new home in Florida and about a year after we moved in, I would be out on the lanai watching TV and my wife would be in the living room when a silhouette of a lady passed in from of the TV screen. She had red hair and was wearing a silver nightgown. This went on for a couple of weeks. I didn't mention this to my wife, but about six months later I mentioned to her that I thought we had a spirit in the home.

She said "I know, she has red hair and wears a silver nightgown." She saw her too and never told me until I mentioned it. After about a year we didn't see her anymore. Maybe she was looking for someone in the wrong house.

I am seventy-eight now and hoping I live the rest of my life with my wife for as long as the mouse in the movie the Green Mile. Life as we know goes on even if it starts out bad.

About the Author

I wrote this book not to dictate to anyone. It's about what you may do to make changes in your life. Teenagers making responsible choices, mothers to hopefully choose the right relationships.

Dads, grandmothers and grandfathers to hopefully set examples of what is right and what is wrong. My hope is that your future is brighter in time as mine is now. Because of my age now, this is my finale, and the book is a catharsis. I am a crossing guard for my country. I control traffic in school zones. It's a challenging experience as most things are.

-Walter Paul Lawrence

Walter Lawrence crossing guard

Matthew Beck Photo Editor
May 12, 2021

Walter Lawrence, a Citrus County crossing guard, directs traffic away from the Inverness Middle School where his post is located. Lawrence's book, "Life of Abuse to Success, a Child's Story," will be published in late May 2021.

Matthew Beck Photo Editor

www.ingramcontent.com/pod-product-compliance
Lightning Source LLC
Chambersburg PA
CBHW031302120626

46545CB00007B/2948